# YOUR KNOWLEDGE HAS VALUE

- - We will publish your bachelor's and master's thesis, essays and papers

- - Your own eBook and book - sold worldwide in all relevant shops

- - Earn money with each sale

Upload your text at www.GRIN.com
and publish for free

**Imprint:**

Copyright © 2016 GRIN Verlag, Open Publishing GmbH
Print and binding: Books on Demand GmbH, Norderstedt Germany
ISBN: 9783668418332

**This book at GRIN:**

http://www.grin.com/en/e-book/356079/self-realization-in-robinson-crusoe-and-robinson-der-juengere

Chao Tang

# Self-Realization in "Robinson Crusoe" and "Robinson der Jüngere"

GRIN Publishing

**GRIN - Your knowledge has value**

Since its foundation in 1998, GRIN has specialized in publishing academic texts by students, college teachers and other academics as e-book and printed book. The website www.grin.com is an ideal platform for presenting term papers, final papers, scientific essays, dissertations and specialist books.

**Visit us on the internet:**

http://www.grin.com/

http://www.facebook.com/grincom

http://www.twitter.com/grin_com

SELF-REALIZATION IN *ROBINSON CRUSOE* AND *ROBINSON DER JÜNGERE*

Chao Tang

Content

1. Introduction

Both *Robinson Crusoe* written by Daniel Defoe and *Robinson der Jüngere* by Joachim Heinrich Campe are published in the eighteenth-century, the so called age of Enlightenment. The Enlightenment thinkers turn their back on the traditional authority of the church and focus on the pursuit of human liberation, rights, natural equality and so on. Later with its root in the thoughts of Enlightenment Individualism developed. When it comes to literature, Defoe's *Robinson Crusoe* creates a new genre of literature: novel. The major difference between novel and previous middle ages' prose fiction is its realism which focuses on individual and particulars while the earlier fiction is in favor of the universal. Self-realization is an essential aspect in understanding the individual realism in novel, because the novel primarily concentrates on individual and self-realization, which is an individual development from a personal inchoate state of being to a state of maturity. Self-realization are "conceptions of selfhood, self-making and self-expression" according to Ryle. It is a process where "fulfillment will be a matter of realizing or giving expression to potentialities pr aspirations that at the same time remain the object of continuous interest, monitoring and readjustment" (24). That is to say that self-realization is not a simple process through which an individual knows himself. It is just the first step of self-realization. After knowing oneself, making changes and finally expressing oneself based on the new identity are crucial to self-realization. In my essay, I will argue that the self-realization of Robinson Crusoe in Defoe's work is missing in Campe's *Robinson der Jüngere* and it shifts to the self-realization of the children in the novel.

2.   Self-Realization in two Robinsonades

From the name of Defoe's novel *Robinson Crusoe,* the German author Johann Gottfried

Schnabel, coined a literary term—Robinsonade—in his book *Die Insel Felsenburg*[1]. The genre

Robinsonade describes the literary works which share a same or similar plot with Defoe's

*Robinson Crusoe*: an individual struggles on an island or in the wildness for his or her own

survival, although the themes, the purposes or the motivations of Robinsonades vary from one to

another. Campe's *Robinson der Jüngere* is a Robinsonade. Based on Defoe's *Robinson Crusoe*

with some changes of plot, narration and characters, Campe's Robinsonade serves for his own

purposes of writing: child education. In the preface of *Robinson der Jüngere,* he mentions and

justifys the reasons why he makes changes to the original Robinsonade. He says that he rewrites

Robinson Crusoe's legend in an amusing way, which he believes that in any other different way

of story telling children would never be so susceptible of useful knowledge. The most important

aim in his book is to show the younger generation events and circumstances to awaken their

consciousness of truth, their pious feeling, and understanding of their own hearts and desires by

transcending important principles of God's and his providence. He also discusses the social

sensational problem at the time which he referrs as "Empfindsamkeitsfieber". He believes this

plague is able to pass to the younger generation through the adults which will cause numbness,

apathy, and dissatisfaction towards the world. He dedicates himself in this book in order to

provide a remedy to the "Empfindsamkeitsfieber", which is able to eventually evoke people's,

especially the younger's gratification and natural desire.

---

[1] See the preface of Schnabel, Johann Gottfried, *Die Insel Felsenburg.* Nordhausen: Johann
Heinrich Groß Buchhändlern, 1731. Print.

According to Hohendahl's argument, literary works which can be marked as "empfindsam" are the works which "in merklicher Befreiung vom Klassizismus dem Einzelnen und seiner Innerlichkeit größere Aufmerksamkeit schenkt und dabei auf die Idividuation des Gefühls größeren Wert legt als auf die allgemein menschlichen Affekte".[2] "Empfindsame Verhalten zum Gefühl", the sentimental behaviors towards feeling, defined by Campe as capable and inclined to find gentle and soft sentiment and proficiency of sympathetic emotional enjoyment. The enjoyment refers to "Gemütsbewegung", mind movement, not objective behaviors. An individual must inwardly experience the objects. The sentimentality, so called "Empfindsamkeit", generates the dialectic of feelings--the relationship between emotion and awareness. Pain is not sentimental but the awareness (1-2). The unrealistic emotion caused by objects is the "Empfindsamkeitsfieber" discussed by Campe. And he supposes that people should be careful in choosing books for children (Campe 397), since the fancy and exaggerated descriptions in books are capable for causing unrealistic emotion. In oder to overcome the "Empfindsamkeitsfieber", one must have the correct awareness. If an individual is not able to realize himself correctly, his awareness and self-expression is problematic. In *Robinson Crusoe,* Robinson's unawareness of his impetuosity and fanaticism towards voyages shows the necessity of Robinson's self-realization. He later gains correct self-realization during his life on the island. To some degree, from the unawareness to awareness of certain things, it is the process of self-realization. The unawareness can be an recognition of a wrong value, incorrect awareness in other words, or it can be the lack of awareness. In the latter situation, it means that the subject's awareness has not developed yet. In *Robinson Crusoe*, it is the first case. Robinson's self-realization is the process

---

2 In noticeable liberation from classicism, (the sentimental literature) gives greater attention to the individual and his inwardness, and greater emphasis on the feelings of individual than on the general human affects

from the incorrect awareness to the correct. And in Campe's work, he focuses on the prevention of the incorrect self-realization of children towards God and morality and sets a strict frame to lead the younger generation to appropriate awareness by using Robinson Crusoe's story. He wants children to have the correct awareness before any other negative effects have come to them.

2.1 Effects of narrative on self-realization

One of the most obvious differences between *Robinson Crusoe* and *Robinson der Jüngere* is their narrative form. In *Robinson Crusoe* Defoe uses first-person narrative in comparison with Campe's third-person narrative. Narrative has considerable effects on realism in novel and thus affects the self-realization.

Watt in *The Rise of the Novel* argues that realism is "the defining characteristic that differentiates the work of early eighteenth-century novelists from previous fiction". Modern realism, unlike the classical and medieval heritage of universals, "begins from the position that truth can be discovered by the individual through his senses". The primary task of novelists is "to convey the impression of the fidelity to human experience", says Watt. Firstly, the arrangement of plot is more spontaneously from individual sense of what his protagonists might plausibly to the next. Secondly, the characteristic of figures in novels presents a rejection of universals and the emphasis on particulars, which can be seen from the name of characters, specific description of time and place of their personal experience. Lastly, at the language level, classical critical tradition in general has no use for the unadorned realistic description (9-34). Because of the realism shown in Defoe's *Robinson Crusoe*, it is regarded as the beginning of the modern novel. What makes Robinson Crusoe's story realistic is revealed from the three aspects discussed by Watt. From the perspective of plot arrangement, Defoe's story naturally follows the time line of

Robinson's life, instead of the development of society or like medieval stories' plot: segments jump from one hero to another. Secondly, Defoe focuses only on the particular life of Robinson, not a group of people, describing his story by using a specific time period and location. It presents its emphasis on individual. In the end, the natural language, like the close description of Robinson's physical work, that Defoe uses makes readers believe that Robinson is a not an extraordinary or a fancy figure, but a common one among us with his particulars. Defoe uses first-person narrative to reveal Crusoe's astonishing experience in his entire life. The narrative shortens the distance between the story teller and the readers. We read the book as if Crusoe himself is telling the story directly to us. The effect of himself telling the story is that it increases the credibility of the story itself and makes the story realistic. And it is crucial to Robinson's self-realization. Because self-realization is a gradual process happened inside of someone's mind, and the information obtained directly from Robinson is the most plausible one in order to analyze his realization.

For instance, in *Robinson Crusoe*, the journal that he writes when he still has ink at the beginning of his life on the island is one of the most essential first-hand materials, because when Robinson writes himself a journal, especially when he is alone on the island, there is no reason for him to exaggerate what he has seen and done at the period of time when he has totally no idea if he is able to escape from the island or even make a long-term survival. Moreover, his inner monologues, especially when he is in the immediate danger, is another critical part of his self-realization. These monologues present us his most natural and unaffected thoughts. For example, when he had his first severe illness on the island, he was desperate and has no idea when death is going to approach him. He says:"not knowing what to do, all this while I had not the least serious religious thought, nothing but the common, Lord ha'mercy upon me, and when it was over, that went away to" (Defoe 65). Because of his critical situation, there is thus no reason to doubt that he is originally impious.

On the contrary, in Campe's *Robinson der Jüngere*, he uses third-person narrative. Instead of Robinson himself narrating his story, the father gathers the children and tells what happened to Robinson. Because the father is not telling the story directly to the readers and with his specific educational goals aimed at his own kids, the distance between readers and Robinson is objectively extended by the form of the narration. Readers are not able to get Robinson's original thoughts, ideas and views. In terms of plot arrangement, instead of continuously telling the story, Robinson's adventure is cut into pieces by the father's explanations, children's questions and family activities. Therefore Robinson's experience is not as real as it is in Defoe's work. For instance, on page 49, the father explains the question raised by one of the childern, Johanns, from the aspect of teaching religious principles "Aber warum mogte Gott auch wohl den Robinson allein erretten, da er die andern Leute alle ertrinken ließ?"[3] (Campe 47), another child, Diederich, asks:"**Dachte Robinson** jezt auch so?"[4]. The father answers:

*Ja; jezt, da er aus so großer Lebensgefahr errettet war, und da er von allen Menschen sich nun verlassen sah: jezt fühlte er in dem Innersten seines Herzens, wie unrecht er gehandelt habe; jezt bat er auf seinen Knien Gott um Vergebung seiner Sünden; jezt sezte er sich fest vor, sich von ganzem Herzen zu bessern und nie wieder etwas zu thun, wovon er wüste, daß es nicht recht wäre.*[5] (Campe 49)

---

[3] But why God preferred to save Robinson alone while he let the rest of them drown?

[4] Did Robinson think in the same way?

[5] Yes; now, because he was saved from grave life danger and saw that all the people had left: now, he felt from bottom of his heart how incorrectly that he has done; on his knees and asked for God's forgiveness of his sins; made strong resolution that he would sincerely remedy his hart and would not do things which he found incorrect anymore.

At the first sight of the father's answer, it seems to be plausible and logical for Robinson to have such thoughts and reactions after being left alone on the island when the rest of the crew is dead. However, does this feeling really comes from Robinson's deepest heart that he should have not started the voyage? Or the father wants to warn his children not to do similar thing like what Robinson has done? And additionally, to Diederich's question, does Robinson think the reason why God only saved him in the same way in which the father explains purely based on his goal of education? The answer is uncertain. Throughout Campe's work, there are many passages where Robinson ideas are modified or even replaced by the fathers words to children. Without the direct information of Robinson's thoughts the self-realization cannot be a complete process.

Why the first-hand inner monologue plays an essential role in the self-realization? Because self-realization is a actively moving circulation. During the procedure of knowing world, people encounter all kinds of events and difficulties and based on human's subjective creativity we solve problems, although it may not be perfect at the first or the first several attempts. Then in retrospect, we exam the actions and the effects and thus in the future based on these experience it is possible to achieve higher and better accomplishments. From action to reflection, and then to further action, people realize the value of subject, laws of nature, better solutions to certain problems, etc. The principle is tantamount to Robinson's situation. Only with a complete combination of his *own* thoughts and actions, it is possible for us to discover his process of self-realization. But in Campe's book, Robinson's action and experience without his inner monologue cut this circulation into segments.

Although Robinson's self-realization is missing in Campe's Robinsonade, the third-person narrative makes the self-realization of the children possible to analyze. If we look back to Watt's argument about realism, firstly, there is a continuous plot arrangement of the father telling the story, day by day, step by step, educating the younger; secondly, it describes a specific family in a specific period of time in a particular place; lastly the language that Campe uses is unadorned and natural which can be seen from the above quoted children's question—direct and simple. All these features match Watt's analysis of realism in novel. The individual object reflected in Campe's Robinsonade is the family. To readers, because of the third-person narrative, Robinson's experience is unreal, but to the children who are the major concern of Campe, their father's narration of story, answers of question, instruction of activities are real. Like we can use the information told by Robinson Crusoe to discover his self-realization, the children use the information taught by their father to accomplish their self-realization.

The shift from first-person narrative in *Robinson Crusoe* to the third-person narrative in Campe's Robinsonade makes the realism switch from Robinson's experience to the children and thus makes the self-realization change from Robinson to the children.

2.2 Distinctions of plots and Robinson's characteristics

*Robinson Crusoe* and *Robinson der Jüngere* have different plot arrangements and characteristic settings, although both of the general stories share a slew of similarities. Campe didn't simply change the narrative form in the new Robinsonade, instead he rearranges the plot and resets the characteristics of Robinson in order to serve his educational purposes. However, these seemingly subtle differences have noticeable influences on the self-realization.

In *Robinson Crusoe,* Defoe describes Robinson's experiences before the ship wreck in a relative long section, including how Robinson's father persuades him not going outside to take adventures and how he struggles in taking his advice and fights against for his desire of voyage. There are three adventures before the ship wreck: the first one is from Hull to London; the second includes two trips from England to Africa, captured as a slave in Moors during the second trip and finally escaped; the last one is to Brazil after he has escaped. After every misfortunate adventure, there is his repentance to what he has done which caused series of affliction. During his first trip to London, when the wind begins to blow he feels inexpressibly sick in his body, he starts thinking:

*I began now seriously to reflect upon what I have done, and how justly I was overtaken by the judgement of Heaven for my wicked leaving my father's house, and abandoning my duty; all the good counsel of my parents, my father's tears and my mother's entreaties came now fresh into my mind...I made many vows and resolutions...if ever I got once my foot upon dry land again, I would go directly home to my father, and never set it in to a ship again while I liv'd...* (Defoe 9)

However, later in London Robinson falls acquainted with a Master of ship who has been on the cost of Guinea, and he cannot resist the offer that the Master provides: no expense for trip, being his companion and all advantage of trade, then he starts his second adventure. It presents the disturbance of the society which overcomes his initial realization of going home. Had been resolute to any of his repentances after any of the miseries, Robinson would not have experienced twenty eight years life alone on the island. But on the other hand, it shows the necessity of his self-realization under a pure nature circumstance without the social disturbance since he can't resist social enticements, the captain's offer for example, and thus can't finish his self-realization under the social circumstance.

Campe, however, keeps only one trip to London that Robinson had before the shipwreck. Even the only one kept adventure is greatly shortened by Campe. He immeasurably abbreviates all the persuasion of Robinson's parents, and totally deletes the rest of his voyages and the repentance. Right after Robinson's first voyage, the plot leads readers to the shipwreck and his lonely life begins, from which Robinson's obstinacy is not able to be shown. The necessity of his self-realization, in other words, the necessity of his further adventures and later being left on the island, is missing from the plot level.

Because Campe noticeably shortens the plot of adventures before the shipwreck in his Robinsonade, the initial image of Robinson is thus not fully developed as it is in the original text. Defoe's Robinson in the beginning of the story, although stubborn, has gained abundant knowledge during his adventure to different places. After his first London trip, he meets a Master of the ship and takes journey with him. He says "I got a competent knowledge of the mathematics and the rules of navigation, learned how to keep an account of the ship's course, take an observation, and, in short, to understand some things that were needful to be understood by a sailor". Also he said that the captain would like to teach and he would like to learn (Defoe 15-16).

But in Campe's description, Robinson is a young man who was ignorant, grew up with his parents' injudicious love, and "hatte seine meiste Zeit mit Herumlaufen zugebracht."[6] (Campe 22). With his naivety, Robinson starts his first trip to London and is left on the island after the trip. Because of the change of the plot in Campe's work, there is no chance for Robinson to develop a more sophisticated and mature personality and learn new knowledge in different fields. Campe's Robinson is like a piece of blank paper on which everyone or himself can easily draw any picture once he has a pen. And this pen is an opportunity for him to calm down, to live without the disturbance of the society and to consider about his genuine and natural desires, namely a chance for his self-realization. For example, in Campe's Robinsonade immediately after he is left alone on the island he "Vor Freud' und Schrekken zitternd warf er sich auf die Knie, hob seine Haende gen Himmel, und dankte mit lauter Stimme, und unter einem Strom von Traenen,

---

6 Spent most of his time in doing nothing

dem Herrn des Himmels und der Erde, der ihn so wunderbar errettet hatte"[7] (Campe 46), it shows Robinson's instant repentance in the book while in Defoe's work even when Robinson has an severe illness after a while he was on the island, he doesn't sincerely think about God at all. That is to say, his process of self-realization is much easier and faster, or even missing, than Defoe's Robinson since the latter has to wipe out what has already drawn on the paper before painting a new one. With the conflicts between Robinson's old views of the world and the outside power pushing his procedure of self-realization, Defoe's *Robinson Crusoe* is more tense and exciting.

If we take a step back to Campe's preface of his Robinsonade where his purposes of rewriting Robinson's story are stated, it is reasonable for him to simplify the plots and draw an innocent image of Robinson at the beginning of the plot. For his educational purposes, there has to be someone who grows up with parents' injudicious love, learning nothing in his youth, being venerable and finally gets punished by life. Campe uses Robinson to build an anti-example for the younger generation and shows negative effects of Robinson doing so. In the end, Robinson still gets a chance to leave the island and return to the civilization. From the aspect of education it is proper and prudent to keep the Defoe's original ending. Because everyone makes different mistakes and for those who have already stepped onto the wrong way of their life, their parents are able to use the story to tell their children that even Robinson is saved in the end, if they repent and take actions to correct what they have already done, they are also forgivable and able to be saved.

Although Campe deletes many of Robinson's adventures and draws a naive image of Robinson, which weakens his self-realization, he creates scenes where children do activities and learn from

---

[7] With joy and fear he quaveringly got on his knees, raised his hands to the heaven, thanked God of the heaven and the earth who amazingly saved him with loud voice and flood of tears.

their father. Children doing outdoor activities is a parallel of Robinson's adventure and their learning procedure is parallel to Crusoe's procedure of knowledge acquisition. In the thirteenth evening, the father talks about Robinson's decision of cutting a bread-fruit tree, instead of directly telling his children the answer, he divides them into two groups and asks them to discuss their own opinions. He sets up a situation which Robinson has gone through and uses it for children's active learning.

Again because of a series of changes of plot and Robinson's characteristic, the self-realization seen on Robinson Crusoe in the original Robinsonade appears on the children in Campe's work.

2.3 Different aspects in the self-realization in two Robinsonades

The self-realization in *Robinson Crusoe* is more complex than it is in *Robinson der Jüngere*. In the former, the self-realization of Robinson Crusoe consists of multifaceted aspects: Robinson's realization on money, work preparation, God and so on. Capme puts the aspect of God's principle and providence in the center and they are the result for children's self-realization: submitting themselves to correct religious principles. Children learn knowledge from their father and do activities under the instruction given by the father in order to complete the self-realization. By analyzing different aspects in two books, we are able to observe how the subjects finish their self-realization differently.

Unlike Campe's Robinsonade, God is not in the middle of Robinson's self-realization in Defoe's work. There are many factors that support Robinson's survival and he learns from many different aspects and later gets aware of the truth of these facets. For instance, money is one of the important concepts in Defoe's Robinsonade: from the beginning of the story to the end, money is throughout Robinson's life, no matter back in England, on his trips, alone on the island or in the end back to the civilization. Amory Dwight Mayo writes in his book, an American educator, "money is alway the same: the representatives of the uses of the world to the human soul...

(money) runs to and fro over charmed cord that unites the soul and world; passing from hand to

hand, it transmits earthly necessities, comforts, luxurious, hopes, energies..." (122). This is

exactly what money brings to Robinson during his self-realization. At first, Robinson wants to

make money to get independent from his family. At this moment, without much money, an offer

for free voyage is enough for him to make the decision to leave his family. His recognition of

money stays at the lowest necessity level: he doesn't think about how dangerous it can be for

someone like himself without any experience to go on board. Even for his second voyage, the

Master of the ship whom he meets in London offers him to "go the voyage with him I should be

at no expense" and gives him advice in overseas trade, Robinson makes the exact the same

decision—"I embraced the offer" (Defoe 16). After his initial success in Brazil in running a

plantation, his attitude towards money changes: "...being a rich and thriving man in my new

plantation, only to pursue a rash and immoderate desire of rising faster than the nature of the

thing admitted..." (Defoe 32), it shows that he is not content about having money for his

necessities any more and wants to reach a comfort or even a luxury level. It is the major reason

why he goes on a trip of salve trade and eventually is left on the island. Since then, his

recognition of money starts changing again. Right after the shipwreck, he takes some tools,

clothing, firearms, etc., from the ship that he took. Among these stuff there are gold and silver,

instead of throwing them away, he keeps them well. Even after he realized "what art thou good

for? Thou art not worth to me-no, not the taking off the ground; one of those knives is worth all

this heap" (Defoe 47), he stores them in his place. It is reasonable for him to take money right

after the shipwreck since his attitude hasn't changed; he still considers that they are valuable at

the first sight. But why he doesn't abandon them and why he takes money again from another wrecked ship after he has realized the useless features of money in his situation? The only possible explanation is that money as a symbol of civilization provides him with hope and energy while he was alone. Looking at them makes him recall the society where he used to live and thus supports him, holding the idea of escaping from the island. In the end of story, he calculates every penny that should belong to him or he owes even after so many years the old plantation has made him richer than ever. He pays all the debt, claims all his property and makes decent plans for the proper usage. Till now, his self-realization of money is completed.

There are also many other aspects from which we are able to analyze his self-realization, and each of them is not less complicated than the his realization of money. Therefore, God plays an important role in his self-realization but not the major role. Even Robinson himself admits in his June 21st journal, when he prayed to God for the first time since he was left on the island he scarcely knew what he said.

On the contrary, principles of God and morality are in the middle of the self-realization in *Robinson der Jüngere*. Rüdiger Steinlein argues that Campe's Robinsonade sets an important literary model for instruction of reality and morality, which ceaselessly endeavors to transmit the correct concepts of God. Through the planed fictionality (change of plot and characteristics of Robinson, discussed above) Campe applies the aim of religious and moral education in his book. The father as the teller of Robinson's story is the "tutor narrator" (Erzieher Erzähler), catering for giving moral comments, God-fearing sensation, and making natural events beneficial for children. The God-like father works as the concretization of the principle of God's providence, but the importance of the hero figure, Robinson, grows not as much as the father. Campe only uses Robinson as a tool to achieve his educational goals. Robinson is simply a project of the father's demonstration. The God-like father is the most essential figure in terms of child education. The intensity of the religious language shows its importance, which in other children literature can hardly be seen. This presentation, according to Steinlein, provides the antidote for the tiresome sensational plague caused by other fancy, eloquent literature.

It is the third reason which explains that Robinson's self-realization in *Robinson der Jüngere* is missing. Robinson only serves as an object in order to get the children self realized. And this is the reason why Campe removes Robinson's original stubbornness from *Robinson Crusoe,* because there is no need for children to know the misleading attitudes of Robinson before the shipwreck in Defoe's work and it has better educational effect by depicting Robinson as a vulnerable person who repents immediately after his faults.

In *Robinson der Jüngere,* there is a positive outcome of the education with the father's absolute rights of explanation of God's principle and his authority, which we can see from the very beginning of the book: On the second page of *Robinson der Jüngere,* there is a picture, depicting the everyday scenes of the father telling his children Robinson's story. The father sits in the middle, leaning on the tree, at the highest point of the ground, while the mother and children sit next and lower to him. It shows the hierarchy in the family and the father is at the top. As for the outcome, it is positive because the father successfully attracts the young people by telling them Robinson's story along with the religious and moral principles. The father uses thirty one days to tell the story and in the thirtieth evening there is a short conversation between Nikolas, Gotlieb and the father:

*Nikolas: Jezt ist mir immer bange, wenn Vater erzählen will.*

*Vater: Wovon denn, lieber Nikolas?*

*Nikolas: Davor, dass die Geschichte bald aus sei.*

*Gotlieb: Wenn ich in Vaters Stelle wäre, ich wolte sie so lang machen! o so lang, dass sie bis Ewigkeit fortdauerte.* [8]

It demonstrates that the children are intoxicated in the learning process and actively ask for it. The positive outcome presents the children's self-realization of religion and morality. Throughout the story, when the father explains certain God's providence, moral principles, if they are not able to understand, they ask their father questions. At this moment, they are undergoing the process of self-realization. For example, in the eighth evening when the father tells them that Robinson has caught llamas and Gotlieb asks him: "Da hätte er sie doch auch müssen gehen lassen, das arme Thier hattte ihm ja nichts gethan".[9] But the father explains that it is lawful to use the animal as human's necessity as long as they are not tortured. Moreover, the children are not only passively listen to their father's explanation, instead, the father also leads them to practice actively. Without telling Robinson has perished, he asks the children to write letters to him. Through this activity, the children discover their genuine sentimentality hidden deeply in their heart and express sympathy. This is a part of their learning progress and self-realization and an epitome of Campe's antidote to the sensational plague that he provides in his book. The last sentence of the book, after the father finishes the story and his educational discourse, all the young people say:"so wil ich es auch machen!".[10] They will do what their

---

[8] Nikolas: Now I am always anxious when father wants to tell the story.
Father: Why then, dear Nikolas?
Nikolas: Because the story is going to end soon.
Gotlieb: If I was father, I would make the story very long. Oh, so long that it forever lasts.

[9] He must let the llama go, the poor animal has done anything to him.

[10] I will do likewise as well.

father told them—religiously and morally correct things. Till now their self-realization is complete.

3. Conclusion

It is obvious to witness Robinson's self-realization in Defoe's Robinsonade due to the various effects of his story telling, such as the effects of first-person narrative, more complex plot and image of Robinson and the multi-faced aspects from which Defoe creates his major character. As for the self-realization in Campe's *Robinson der Jüngere,* based on Campe's educational goals towards the younger generation and his understanding in the sensational plague at that time, he creates a relative structured narrative form in order to set a line for children. He carefully keeps the children in the line and eliminates the side effects that may potentially do harm to the younger. Unlike the original Robinson story where Robinson uses all kinds of tools and experiences different events and then finishes his self-realization, Campe sets Robinson as a tool and uses him to have the children done different activities along with the father's educational discourse and finish their self-realization. The doer of the self-realization switches from Robinson to the children.

The aspect of self-realization is one of the crucial aspects in understanding and analyzing both *Robinson Crusoe* and *Robinson der Jüngere* except for christian conversion, colonial culture and so on. In the fifteenth-century people held fear towards nature. They believed that people would be tangled or distracted in the nature because of the control of the church. However, the situation has flipped: In 18th-century, in Rousseau's notion, one of the major problems in the German society was that people were corrupted by the civilization and they should seek a kind of independence from social entanglements, be "natural", be self-directing, and attend to our emotions as more "natural" guides to life (Pinkard 11). People in the eighteenth-century started to realize the problem of society and civilization at that time and pay more attention back to nature created by God in order to seek the sense of peace and get self-realized. One may take self-realization into consideration while reading novels in the eighteenth-century.

Bibliography

Campe, Joachim Heinrich, and Alwin Binder. *Robinson Der Jüngere: Zur Angenehmen Und Nützlichen Unterhaltung Für Kinder*. Stuttgart: Reclam, 2012. Print.

Defoe, Daniel, and John J. Richetti. *Robinson Crusoe*. London: Penguin, 2003. Print.

Hohendahl, Peter Uwe. *Der Europäische Roman der Empfindsamkeit*. Planegg: Koch Buchverlag, 1982. Print.

Mayo, Amory Dwight. *Symbols of the Capital; or, civilization in New York*. New York: Thatcher & Hutchinson, 1859. Print.

Pinkard, Terry. *German Philosophy: 1760- 1860 The Legacy of Idealism*. Cambridge: University press, 2002. Print.

Ryle, Martin, and Kate Soper. *To Relish the Sublime? Culture and Self-Realization in Postmodern Times*. London: Verso, 2002. Print.

Steinlein, Rüdiger. "'Aufgeklärte Gottesfrucht', das Gott-Vater-Paradigma als religionspädagogisches und wirkungsästhetisches Prinzip erzählender Kinder- und Jugendliteratur der Aufklärung am Beispiel von J.H. *Campus Robinson der Jüngere*." *Zeitschrift für Germanistik 4*: H.1. 7-23.

Watt, Ian. *The Rise of Novel: Studies in Defoe, Richardson and Fielding*. Berkeley: University of California Press, 1957. Print.